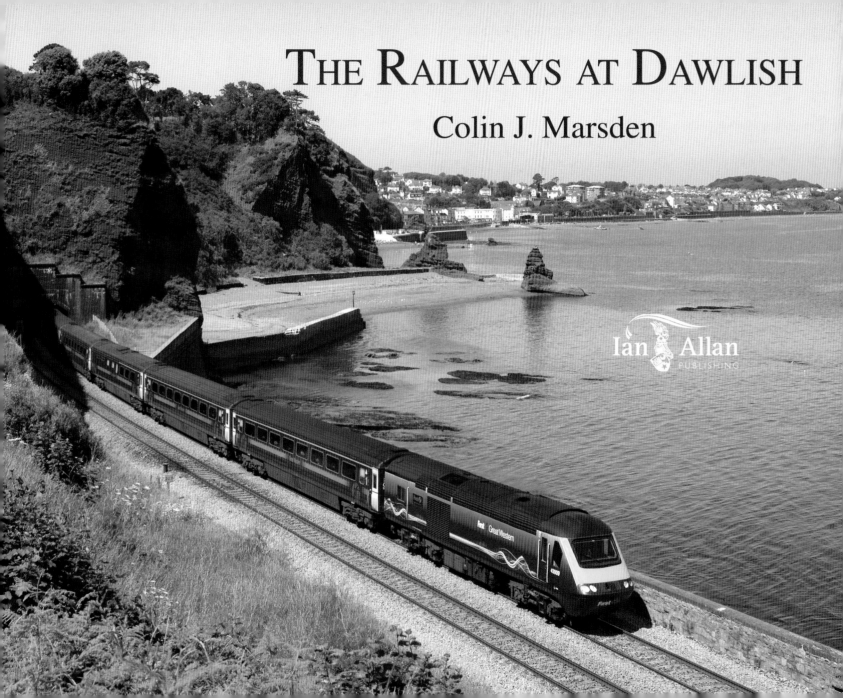

THE RAILWAYS AT DAWLISH

Colin J. Marsden

Ian Allan
PUBLISHING

Introduction

There is probably no other railway location in the world which attracts the same level of interest as the 22-mile section of the former Great Western main line between Exeter and Newton Abbot in South Devon, traversing the hugely popular and ever photogenic Sea Wall through Dawlish and Teignmouth. This album, *The Railways at Dawlish,* has been produced to show the route, scenery and above all diversity of train types seen traversing the Sea Wall over the last 40 or so years.

Built by the South Devon Railway in 1846 and originally operated using atmospheric 'power' for propulsion, the line was eventually absorbed into the Great Western Railway and converted into a conventional railway, firstly as the Great Western Railways Broad Gauge (7ft ½in) and later converted in May 1892 to standard gauge (4ft 8½in).

From Exeter St Davids station, around one mile from the centre of the city, the route heads west through the suburb of St Thomas and heads for Exminster, where the line starts to parallel the River Exe, the waterway gradually opens out and the water and rail route progress with the open sea coming into view as the train passes through Dawlish Warren. This section of the route offers some wonderful views of the East Devon estuary towns of Topsham and Lympstone, before the major holiday destination of Exmouth is viewed opposite Dawlish Warren. Between Starcross and Dawlish Warren is one of the most photographed railway locations in the world - Cockwood Harbour.

From Dawlish Warren, the Sea Wall proper starts, with a footpath hugging the line as far as Dawlish, this section includes locations such as Langstone Rock and the Rockstone Bridge, popular names found in many railway photographic captions.

The Sea Wall, now maintained by Network Rail, is a constant cause of concern to the rail industry, with frequent closures during the winter months due to rough seas, high tides and ballast washouts. Most years, sections of the walkway portion of the wall are washed away with frequent adverse comments about Dawlish and the Sea Wall made in newspapers, the TV media and comics throughout the world.

The town of Dawlish, roughly central between Exeter and Newton Abbot, and home to the author of this book for 20 years, is still a delightful seaside town. With a population of around 13,000 it is still small enough to have almost village life, while in the summer months the population rises 30 fold, with huge camp and leisure sites surrounding the town.

The area around Dawlish provides little option for every visitor to see the railway at very close quarters; the station is literally located on the edge of the beach with a Great Western-designed viaduct spanning the main seafront. Views of the railway and indeed most of Lyme Bay can be obtained from numerous viewpoints, these are especially impressive from Lea Mount, located on the west side of the town, where many walkways on the red sandstone cliffs offer endless views of the line.

By virtue of the land contours, the Sea Wall path only extends to the area of the first tunnel west of Dawlish-Coryton; from here, those wishing to walk westward need to climb the cliff path and walk along the main Teignmouth Road as far as Smugglers Lane in Holcombe, where a narrow road/path leads down to the railway and starts the eastern end of the Teignmouth Sea Wall and pathway, again giving uninterrupted views of the railway as far as Teignmouth station.

Between Dawlish and Teignmouth are five tunnels through the sandstone rocks; again these cause major headaches for maintenance with a constant risk of rock falls. Consideration has been given on many occasions to 'daylight' some of these tunnels, but thankfully this has so far not been done.

At Teignmouth the rail route turns slightly inland to bypass the town which is located between the station and sea front. Shortly after the town, the line passes the Port of Teignmouth and leaves the open sea, now following the River Teign inland through Bishopsteignton and on towards Newton Abbot.

Newton Abbot was once a thriving railway town, with a carriage and wagon workshop, locomotive works, and running depot. The town was the junction for the branch to Mortonhampstead, Haytor and Exeter through Christow via Heathfield and the junction for passengers between the Paignton and Plymouth lines. Today, just three platform faces remain at Newton Abbot, with the branch now truncated at Heathfield and is little more than a siding, the former workshop site is now industrial units.

Just west of Newton Abbot is Aller; this was once Aller Junction, the physical split between the Torquay/Paignton and Totnes/Plymouth lines but, alas, today this is just a diverging point, with the actual rail split being close to Newton Abbot.

Over the years the 'Sea Wall' has seen a huge diversity of train types; the author has for many years collected illustrations of trains passing Dawlish and a total of nearly 200 different classes, sub-classes and types have been recorded. When the steam and diesel-hydraulic eras passed into history, many thought the magic of trains on the Sea

First published 2007

ISBN (10) 0 7110 3253 X
ISBN (13) 978 0 7110 3253 8

Published by Ian Allan Publishing

an imprint of Ian Allan Publishing Ltd, Hersham, Surrey KT12 4RG.
Printed in England by Ian Allan Printing Ltd, Hersham, Surrey KT12 4RG.

Code: 0705/B

Visit the Ian Allan Publishing website at www.ianallanpublishing.com

Wall would end. In fact, it seems to be the opposite; the diversity of classes, operators and liveries, boosted by the high number of special and charter trains traversing the route generates a huge interest, with few days passing without some form of unusual happening being recorded.

Although over the last 30 years I have authored over 60 railway titles, without doubt this product has given me the greatest pleasure to produce. The diversity of illustrations available is truly amazing and it has been hugely difficult to include all the 'must have' pictures. I do hope that readers and viewers will have as much pleasure looking through its pages and share some of the enjoyment of trains traversing the 'Sea Wall' section. Literally thousands of enthusiasts and photographers visit the route every year; some have eventually moved to the area to be closer to the rail route they enjoy and many of these visitors and 'locals' have become friends and acquaintances over the years, either sharing photographic time in the many locations or having a glass of the finest local ale in my Dawlish local 'The Laffinn Pig' and, needless to say, talking about trains.

I would like to extend my thanks to the many local people and photographers who have assisted me over the years, especially to Peter Gray, John Lambert, Kevin Wills, members of SWRG and my family Jean Marsden and Wendy Etheridge.

The Author of this title operates the Dawlish Sea Wall website which can be found at www.therailwaycentre.com where many illustrations, history and unusual workings over the sea wall can be found.

Colin J. Marsden
Dawlish
January 2007

Front Cover: Probably the view which most typifies Dawlish and the Sea Wall. Seen from Lea Mount, a down First Great Western HST forms the 07.30 Paddington–Penzance led by power car No 43161 on 14 July 2006, while Virgin 'Voyager' No 221110 passes the station forming the 07.30 Penzance–Glasgow. *Author*

Title Page: Sporting the short-lived First Great Western 'dynamic lines' livery applied to just two power cars and three passenger vehicles for the Greater Western franchise launch on 1 April 2006, Class 43 No 43009 passes Horse Cove, leading the 12.05 Paddington–Paignton summer extra service on 17 June 2006. *Author*

Back Cover: The classic view of Cockwood Harbour, taken on 10 June 2004, shows EWS Class 66/0 No 66190 powering the afternoon St Blazey–Newport Alexandra Dock Junction freight formed of just four vehicles. *Author*

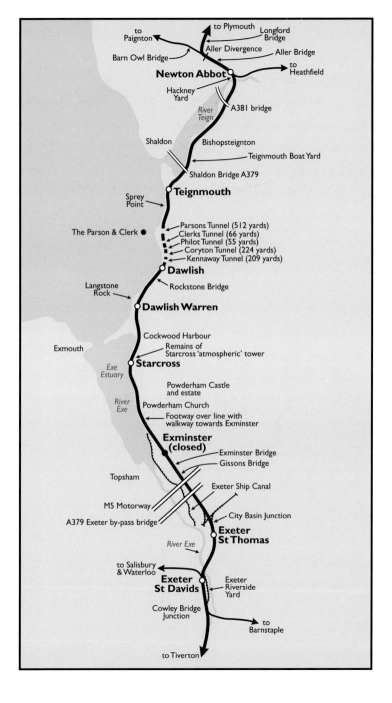

Right: Following the introduction of colour light signalling in the West Country from the mid-1980s, the platform layout at Exeter St Davids was changed, with the principal up/down main line platform faces moving to island platforms of the station and the original down main platform line becoming used mainly for Exeter–Salisbury–Waterloo and Exeter–Exmouth services. Traversing the present down main platform line, Virgin Trains 'Voyager' No 220026 *Stagecoach Voyager* arrives at Exeter St Davids on 28 June 2006 forming the 10.26 Newcastle–Plymouth service. In the distance a South West Trains Class 159 can be seen awaiting to form a Waterloo-bound service. *Author*

Above: One of the most popular classes of diesel locomotive ever to operate in the West Country were the Class 52 'Western' diesel-hydraulics. A total of 74 locomotives of the design were built by BR Workshops at Swindon and Crewe between 1961 and 1964. In the days when around a dozen daily van trains operated through Exeter, formed of general parcels and Royal Mail stock, 'Western' No D1049 *Western Monarch* arrives in the then down main platform with a Bristol-Plymouth parcels service on 16 June 1976, just a few months before the class was finally withdrawn. *Author*

Right: The livery transition from 1960s BR green to the 1967-adopted 'standard' BR rail-blue was a drawn-out affair, with some two-tone green-liveried Class 47s still being active in 1976. On 16 August 1976, No 47195 departs from the down main platform at Exeter St Davids leading the 13.30 Paddington–Penzance service. *Author*

Left: The diversity of train liveries in the West Country that can be seen on the section of line between Exeter St Davids and Newton Abbot, must be one of the highest in the UK. In the early summer of 2006, following the takeover of the new Greater Western franchise by FirstGroup, some shuffling of stock took place, this including the reallocation of ex First TransPennine Express Class 158 No 158750 to Exeter. The set was one of the original batch used by Virgin Trains and still sported Regional Railways colours overlaid with First TransPennine stickers. The set is seen departing from Exeter St Davids on 28 June 2006 forming the 14.57 Barnstaple–Exmouth. *Author*

Right: Crossing from the 'up' line to platform 3 at Exeter St Davids, South West Trains Class 159 No 159007 arrives on 29 June 2006 with the 14.47 Plymouth–Waterloo service. This train changes direction at Exeter and continues to London Waterloo via Exeter Central and Salisbury. *Author*

Above: The diversity of multiple-unit types and liveries that can be found traversing the Exeter-Newton Abbot line seems to be growing all the time, with nationwide reallocations, application of new operator liveries and the use of trains as mobile advertisement hoardings becoming more popular. On 21 July 2006, First Great Western-operated 'Alphaline' Class 158 No 158747, which is fitted with modified snowploughs on the front end, passes under the M5 bridge at Exminster forming the 11.05 Exeter St Davids–Penzance service. This unit carries the name *Richard Trevithick* which includes bodyside-applied pictograms. Following the expansion of FirstGroup operations to include the former Wessex Trains area from April 2006, a new all-over blue livery for local train sets was launched in January 2007. *Author*

Above: The road leading off the Matford round-about between Exeter and Exminster provides a view of trains, but is rather busy for general photography. In full InterCity 'Swallow' livery the 14.45 Penzance–Paddington heads for Exeter on 23 June 1995 led by power car No 43015. *Author*

Right: For around 20 years from the mid-1960s, the Exeter-area local passenger services were in the hands of first-generation DMMU stock, mainly of Class 118, but as years progressed this extended to Classes 101, 108, 120 and 122. On 6 July 1984, blue and grey BR-liveried Class 118 set No P (Plymouth) 462 heads the 14.27 Exeter St Davids–Paignton past the facing points of the soon-to-be-closed Exminster down loop. Until 30 March 1964 a station existed at this location, and in recent years several attempts have been made to have a halt returned to this rapidly expanding suburb of Exeter. *Author*

Above: In recent years freight traffic has not been prolific in the West Country, with only a handful of usually lightly-loaded trains operating each day. These days, motive power is usually confined to Class 66s, but in the past members of Classes 31, 33, 37, 45, 46, 47, 50, 56 and 60 were frequently recorded. On 16 July 2002, EWS No 60089 *The Railway Horse* approaches Exminster and passes below the M5 bridge powering the 08.58 Stoke-on-Trent–St Blazey, formed of just two wagons. *Author*

Right: The view from the farm bridge at Gissons, Exminster offers an excellent view of up trains during the late afternoon and evening. On 16 July 2006, the first of the 2006 season's 'Torbay Express' steam-powered services operated. Led by Great Western 'King' No 6024 *King Edward I*, the train is seen pulling away from the old Exminster station area. *Author*

Above: The former Exminster signalbox, which closed on 15 November 1986, was used for many years as a bird observation area for the adjacent Exminster Marshes which attracts an abundance of diverse bird life. On 15 July 2006, First Great Western's 16.00 Penzance–Paddington service, led by power car No 43151 with No 43148 on the rear, passes through the old Exminster station site, the passenger platforms once being served by loop tracks. *Author*

Left: In the days when general freight traffic was still to be found on the Sea Wall section, Class 31/1 No 31230 approaches Exminster on 4 July 1984 powering the 10.33 Exeter Riverside–Plymouth Friary 'Air Braked Service' (ABS) freight formed of six wagons, ranging from high-capacity china clay to engineering department ballast wagons. *Author*

Above: Enthusiast and charter specials powered by either steam or diesel traction frequently visit the West Country and can be captured traversing the Sea Wall section. One of the more popular preserved locomotives which at the time had Network Rail main-line certification was 'Peak' No 46035, owned by Pete Waterman. On 15 February 2003 it is seen approaching Powderham crossing, heading an 05.10 Crewe–Newton Abbot Pathfinder Railtours charter. The train later returned as far as Bridgend, powered by steam. It is quite evident that the train was well loaded with 'Peak' bashers. *Author*

Right: In the closing years of Virgin Trains' use of Class 47s on CrossCountry duties, a number of locomotives gained celebrity status, with Virgin Trains painting examples in different heritage liveries. One locomotive which gained an almost cult following was No 47840 *North Star*, which was repainted into 1960s BR rail blue with full yellow ends. On 16 July 2002 No 47840 pounds towards Powderham along the banks of the River Exe, powering the 06.05 Derby–Plymouth, formed of a rake of Virgin Trains-liveried Mk2 stock. After arrival in Plymouth the 'celebrity' returned north at the helm of the 11.51 Plymouth–Liverpool Lime Street. This loco is now preserved on the West Somerset Railway. *Author*

Above: The section of line skirting the banks of the River Exe, especially in the Powderham area, has always been a popular location for photographers. Alas, today the lineside vegetation almost prevents the view of trains. On 6 August 1960, a rather tatty-looking Great Western 'Grange' 4-6-0, No 6814 *Enborne Grange* pulls past the Powderham Estate powering the 07.30 Newcastle–Paignton service. *Peter Gray*

Right: As can be seen, the instance of lineside fires caused by passing steam trains is not a new problem to the railway industry. Here, the embankment between Starcross and Cockwood is burning while the 13.20 Paddington-Kingswear passes by, led by Great Western 'Castle' 4-6-0 No 5060 *Earl of Berkeley* on 6 August 1960. The photographer's notes show this train had taken four hours and 25 minutes to reach this spot after departure from London; today a London-West of England express would pass Cockwood around two hours and 20 minutes after departure. *Peter Gray*

Above: A wonderful period transport picture, taken in July 1966 between Starcross and Cockwood and showing Class 42 'Warship' No D816 *Eclipse* heading west with a mixed rake of Mk1 and company stock forming the 09.20 Liverpool–Paignton service. On the road a then-new Ford Zephyr and an Austin A35, complete with a well-loaded roof rack carrying holidaymakers' belongings, also head west. The signal above the fourth coach is the up outer home for Starcross. It is also worth noting the period roadsigns. *Peter Gray*

Right: In the days when Cockwood Harbour had three water inlets from the River Exe, train M25, the 17.15 Paignton–Nottingham crosses the well-filled harbour powered by Great Western 'Modified Hall' No 6976 *Graythwaite Hall* on 6 August 1960. At this time it is worth noting that a telegraph line crossed the harbour and a semaphore signal existed on the Dawlish Warren bank. *Peter Gray*

Above: One of the most popular photographic locations between Exeter and Newton Abbot is Cockwood Harbour, located between Starcross and Dawlish Warren and offering some splendid photographic viewpoints during the afternoon and evening. However, it was not every day that three Railfreight Coal-Sector Class 37s could be found at the location. On 2 May 1994 Nos 37799, 37796 and 37896 cross the Harbour powering empty railtour stock from Paignton to Exeter. Class 37s have long been associated with the Sea Wall route, following the demise of diesel-hydraulics. *Author*

Left: With stock transfers to Arriva Trains Wales in 2005, a handful of former Anglia-liveried Class 150s found their way to the west. Set No 150245 passes Cockwood Harbour on 22 June 2005 forming the 14.53 Penzance–Swansea service. Rather a long way, perhaps, to travel on a Class 150, which are not renowned for their comfort or high-quality interiors. *Author*

Above: The twice-weekly Freightliner Heavy Haul-operated cement train from Blue Circle Industries Hope to Moorswater and return, which until early 2006 was formed of both PCA tank cars and ferryvans for the conveyance of bagged cement, always generated local interest, with the up returning empty train traversing the Sea Wall around tea time during the summer. With water in the harbour and sinking light some outstanding photographic results could be obtained from the embankment on the Exeter side of Cockwood Harbour. On 14 September 2004, No 66613 slowly passes Cockwood forming the 15.35 Moorswater–Hope. The terminal at Moorswater is fed off the Liskeard-Looe branch and requires some intricate shunting manoeuvres. On the train's return it usually has to operate west from Moorswater to Par to run around before working north. With changes in the requirement for cement in Cornwall, from early 2006 this train was formed of PCA tank cars only with the train ceasing to run in autumn 2006. *Author*

Above: Often photography at Cockwood Harbour is restricted by the position of the small boats which are moored in the 'inner' harbour area, access to which is by two under-rail bridges, one located at either end and only usable at high tide. With the full introduction of Virgin Trains 'Voyager' units on CrossCountry services, HSTs being deployed on FGW duties and various DMUs on local services, the number of locomotive-hauled trains to record is now very few. On 19 October 2004, this amazing sight was recorded of Class 57/6 No 57602 *Restormel Castle* piloting HST powercar No 43188 leading the 13.46 Penzance–Paddington over the causeway. The train had failed at Penzance and was assisted through to Exeter St Davids. *Author*

Right top: In the summer of 2004, Class 180 stock was rostered to form the 14.35 Paddington–Plymouth for several weeks to enable training of Exeter-based footplate staff on the traction before deployment on a handful of West of England services. On 4 August 2004, sets Nos 180103 and 180104 cross Cockwood Harbour bound for Plymouth. *Author*

Right: On 14 September 2002 a steam-powered charter from Victoria to Plymouth formed of Pullman stock was powered by LNER A3 Pacific No 4472 *Flying Scotsman. En route* the locomotive had to be assisted forward from Exeter St Davids by EWS Class 66 No 66076 which was coupled 'inside' the steam locomotive. This near unprecedented sight is seen from the western bank of Cockwood Harbour during the early afternoon. *Author*

When the Class 50s started operation in the West Country in the mid-1970s, largely to replace the Class 52 'Western' diesel-hydraulic locomotives, the fleet of 50 were despised by enthusiasts, with many refusing to either travel behind the locomotives or photograph them. Things certainly changed, for by the early 1980s a huge number of haulage enthusiasts and photographers flocked to the West Country, especially the Waterloo to Exeter and Sea Wall area, to follow nearly every move the fleet made. After the 'Hoovers', a name derived from the noise the locomotives made under power, were withdrawn, a significant number were preserved. With the privatisation of the UK railways from the mid-1990s, a greater chance emerged of allowing private-owner traction to operate on the national network. Thankfully some of the preserved '50s' were rebuilt to 'Group Standards' and a small number are now authorised to operate at up to 100mph on the Network Rail infrastructure. On 1 October 2005, Nos 50031 *Hood* and 50049 *Defiance* powered the return leg of a charter from Kingswear on the Torbay & Dartmouth Railway to Northampton, which had arrived in the west powered by steam traction. The train is seen passing Cockwood in what can only be described as superb light. *Author*

Above: Until the abolition of mechanical signalling between Exeter and Newton Abbot in autumn 1986 and the introduction of colour light signalling controlled from Exeter Power Signalbox, mechanical boxes remained at Exeter, Exminster, Dawlish Warren, Dawlish, Teignmouth and Newton Abbot during the modern traction era. Dawlish Warren box, with 58 levers, was located at the London end of the down platform and controlled the station area with 'loop' lines on both the up and down side. With the up mainline signal lowered indicating a train was 'on block' from the west, a down Paddington–Newquay SAGA relief train, headed by Class 47/0 No 47235 and formed of Mk1 stock takes the main line through the station. To the rear of Dawlish Warren signalbox is the famous sea turf Dawlish Warren Golf Club, which is reputedly one of the finest golf courses in the area. *Author*

Right: After the withdrawal of diesel-hydraulics from the West Country, a small batch of BR Type 2 Class 25s was drafted to Laira Depot, many of these finding their way onto local Exeter to Paignton/Plymouth services, as well as freight duties and work on the Barnstaple line. On 7 July 1980, Class 25/1 No 25058 awaits departure from Dawlish Warren, with the 16.25 Paignton–Exeter St Davids, formed of four blue and grey-liveried Mk1 coaches. *Author*

Above: In mechanical signalling days, unrefurbished Class 50 No 50027 *Lion* takes the up main track through Dawlish Warren station on 12 June 1980, powering the St Austell to Kensington Olympia 'Motorail' service. This train was formed of 10 Mk1 or 2 coaches and 10 'Motorail' wagons on which up to three motor cars were placed on each. The service has now sadly gone, with most holidaymakers choosing to use road transport to reach the West Country. *Author*

Right: With Staff Association camping coaches located on the up side at Dawlish Warren, unrefurbished Class 50 No 50049 *Defiance* slowly pulls out of the down passenger loop with a rake of empty four-wheel ballast wagons on 23 August 1978. The train had originated at Taunton and was going to Hackney Yard in Newton Abbot. *Author*

Left: The area around Dawlish Warren is the real start of the Dawlish Sea Wall section, with a walkway adjacent to the line from Dawlish Warren station through to Dawlish. Just to the west of Dawlish Warren station a GWR-design footbridge crosses the line, taking pedestrians from the council-operated car park to the sea wall. This bridge also offers some excellent views of the line, one way overlooking Dawlish Warren station and the other, as shown here, towards Langstone Rock. This view is especially good in terms of light during the late afternoon. On 21 June 1981, Class 31/1 No 31165 slows for the facing points to enter the passenger loop at Dawlish Warren forming the 17.50 Paignton–Exeter St Davids service. The train is formed of five Mk1s, a far cry from today's local services either formed of a single-car Class 153 or a two-carriage Class 150/2. *Author*

Right: Probably one of the most photographed views of a railway line in the world is that from Langstone Rock (Dawlish Warren) looking towards Dawlish, showing the wonderful red sandstone cliffs, the railway line and the famous Sea Wall located between the rail tracks and the coastline. Taken from the side of Langstone Rock, a Virgin Trains 'Voyager' service formed of sets No 220011 and 220006 form the 09.30 Paignton–Glasgow train on 24 July 2004. Under the 1980s re-signalling of the West Country, the line between Dawlish Warren and Teignmouth is signalled for down trains to operate over both tracks, but the use of the up line for down trains is usually confined to periods of inclement weather or engineering work. *Author*

Above: The view looking east from Langstone Rock towards Dawlish Warren station is another popular one for photographers. In this picture we see the old order of the day, a 'Western' Class 52 No D1068 *Western Reliance* taking power as it rounds the curve onto the sea wall with the 07.40 Kensington Olympia–St Austell 'Motorail' service on 25 June 1976. *Author*

Right: Today we have one 'preserved' Class 52 authorised for main-line running, No D1015 *Western Champion* owned by the DTG. This locomotive often powers charter services, sometimes to the west. On 9 August 2003, No D1015 rounds Langstone Rock with the 07.25 Paddington–Penzance charter. *Author*

Left: In full First Great Western livery and led by power car No 43134 with No 43186 on the rear, the 08.05 Paddington–Newquay 'Holiday Express' heads for the sea wall on 1 July 2006. *Author*

Above: The tall cliff at Dawlish Warren known as Langstone Rock offers numerous views of the line in both directions; these are best during the morning period when the sun is on the sea side. With the high number of trains traversing the section, especially on summer Saturdays, it is often possible to capture two trains in one frame. On 1 July 2006, de-branded Wessex Trains-liveried Class 150/2 No 150254 traverses the up line and slows for the approach-control signal to take it into the up passenger loop at Dawlish Warren forming the 10.22 Paignton–Exmouth. On the down line Virgin Trains No 221121 *Charles Darwin* heads west with the 06.16 Preston–Plymouth service. *Author*

Left: One thing that privatisation has done for UK railways is provide a diversity of colour to a degree never seen before. Here a charter service heads west at Langstone Rock, powered by Cotswold Rail Class 47s No 47316 *Cam Peak*, painted in Cotswold silver livery, and No 47714 displaying Anglia Turquoise colours. The train is formed of former Virgin Trains Mk3s painted in VT red. This train was one of the first Cotswold charters, departing at 06.00 from Codsall in the West Midlands and running through to Penzance on 1 October 2005. *Author*

Above: The Sea Wall which runs between the rail tracks and the beach offers some excellent views, in places allowing people to get very close to passing trains. With the town of Dawlish in the background and the wooden Rockstone Bridge at the rear of the train, a Virgin Trains 2+7 HST heads for Exeter on 29 June 2002, led by powercar No 43193. The train is the 07.20 Plymouth–Aberdeen. *Author*

Left: The Dawlish and Teignmouth sea walls are subject to an annual battering by the sea which often closes the line in the winter months. This was the view near Langstone Rock in the winter of 1966; the wall has been demolished and rebuilding is in process, while a 'Western'-powered freight passes by on the up line. *Peter Gray*

Right: Steam-powered charters which traverse the Sea Wall are very popular with holidaymakers and locals and usually bring out large crowds. On 1 August 2004 Ex-Great Western 'Castle' No 5051 *Earl Bathurst* starts to apply power at Langstone Rock, forming the 09.00 Bristol Temple Meads–Kingswear 'Torbay Express' charter. *Author*

Left: Midway along the Sea Wall from Dawlish Warren to Dawlish is the Rockstone footbridge, allowing access from the Exeter Road to the beach. The bridge offers an excellent photographic viewpoint and is much favoured by locals and visitors. The name Rockstone is derived from the name of the former hotel which once stood on the Exeter Road adjacent to the footpath leading to the bridge. With light waves lapping onto the foreshore, and with Langstone Rock in the background, First Great Western's 09.05 Paddington–Penzance service, led by powercar No 43168 heads towards Dawlish on 2 April 2005. This set is unusually formed, with its two first-class vehicles at the west end of the formation. Usually the first class carriages are formed at the London end. *Author*

Above: The Rockstone Bridge apart from providing a good vantage point from which to take pictures, can also act as an effective frame for up trains. Passing under the present timber structure on 2 April 2005, Class 43 power car No 43021 leads the 08.04 Penzance–Paddington service. *Author*

Left: Taken some 26 years before the picture above, this view of 'Peak' Class 46 No 46003 passes under the older concrete Rockstone Bridge on 7 June 1979 forming a Plymouth to Leeds service. It is suspected that today's Health & Safety Executive would have something to say about the staff working on the bridge, especially as no protective or high-visibility clothing was being worn and one man was standing on a single bar of scaffolding as trains traversed the line below. When the Rockstone Bridge was rebuilt in the 1980s, the original concrete deck was replaced with a timber structure. *Author*

Above: Since the introduction of Class 159s on the Network SouthEast and later South West Trains route to Waterloo, members of the fleet have traversed the Sea Wall daily with through workings from Waterloo to Paignton/Plymouth and a Summer Saturday service to Brighton. On 2 April 2005 two pairs of '159s' pass at Rockstone Bridge. Nos 159002/014 form the 10.10 Paignton to Brighton, while Nos 159012/009 traverse the down line with the 07.10 Waterloo–Paignton. *Author*

Right: In recent years a number of track and infrastructure test trains have operated, usually in the form of the New Measurement Train or NMT formed of an HST set; however, for a couple of weeks in the summer of 2006 when the HST set was receiving maintenance, a temporary formation was made up with DRS Class 37s Nos 37602 and 37606 either end of four vehicles including test car No 999550. The train is seen on 21 July 2006 passing Rockstone Bridge forming the 10.15 Plymouth–Paddington. *Kevin Wills*

Right: The view over Dawlish station from the Coastguards Bridge, which links Exeter Road with the Sea Wall, offers an excellent view of operations. On 30 June 1978, unrefurbished Class 50 No 50048 *Dauntless* pulls away from Dawlish with the 09.23 Paignton to Paddington service. This view has largely changed with Network Rail building a compound for sea wall maintenance adjacent to the bridge. *Author*

Below: This was the view at Dawlish on the morning of 28 October 2004 after a bad overnight storm placed debris on the line, knocked down fences and saw ballast thrown into Marine Parade, damaging motor vehicles. The line was closed for three days. *Author*

Above: For a couple of years from 1985, some local services in the West Country were taken over by a batch of brown and cream-liveried Class 142 units, known as 'Skipper' stock. These did not operate well in the West and were not welcomed by the travelling public. Problems with overcrowding and technical issues over the wheel/rail interface, especially on lightly-used branch lines, saw the sets transferred away from the area. Passing the semaphore home signal for Dawlish and approaching the Coastguards Bridge, set No 142024 slows for the Dawlish stop on 22 August 1986, forming the 10.55 Exeter St Davids–Newton Abbot service. *Author*

Above: The former Coastguard lookout, located at the London end of Dawlish station is now a bistro and bar and offers some excellent outside seating for train watching. On 8 July 2006, a nine-car Virgin Voyager formation, led by set No 220016 *Midland Voyager* passes by forming the 08.05 Penzance to Newcastle summer Saturday holiday train. The footbridge above the train is what is known as the Coastguards footbridge, while the building on the left is the former home of the Coastguards boat, with a slipway in front leading down to the beach. In the background is Dawlish platform. *Author*

Above: While the general landscape of this view of Dawlish has not changed much in the last 32 years, the area in the right foreground now sports office accommodation for Network Rail local sea wall maintenance operations and thus blocks this view from being taken today. In August 1974, 'Hymek' No D7017 (now preserved on the West Somerset Railway) hauls an up Plymouth Friary to Exeter freight formed of clay hood and bitumen wagons. *Chris Perkins*

Above: The view looking towards Exeter from the Coastguard footbridge in Dawlish provides an excellent vista of the line and bay, and even in rough seas offers some protection for the photographer and observer to watch operations. Carrying a stencil reporting number V93, the 09.05 Liverpool Lime Street–Plymouth heads west on 17 September 1960 adjacent to a very angry sea. Power is provided by Great Western 'Castle' 4-6-0 No 4073 *The South Wales Borderers*. The view today from this location has not changed a lot; the semaphore signal has obviously gone and the little footbridge from the wall to Sea Lawn Terrace is no longer present, but the rest of the view remains basically the same. *Peter Gray*

Above: One of the most recognisable views of the Dawlish area is that of a train between Dawlish station and Kennaway Tunnel, although many items have changed since this view was taken on 27 August 1961. The same view cannot be taken today, as the fence on the land side of the railway has now been replaced with an ugly 6ft black steel structure. The signals have sadly gone, but the station fabric remains the same. In perfect afternoon light, Great Western 28xx 2-8-0 No 2882 has a good head of steam as it heads west with a mixed freight, probably bound for Plymouth from Avonmouth. It is interesting to note that the up and down signals were located on the opposite side of the line to which they apply, thus improving signal sighting for footplate staff. *Peter Gray*

Above: The entire Sea Wall route from Exeter to Newton Abbot receives a huge amount of maintenance, especially the section in the vulnerable area between the Exe estuary and the River Teign. In periods of bad weather when the wall is battered by southern winds, washouts can occur and ground staff have to keep a 24-hour watch on the open sections to ensure total safety. Over the years much has been written about building an inland diversionary route from Exeter to Newton Abbot, but the huge cost of construction together with capital investment would make this totally uneconomic. In November/December 2005 several weekends of track replacement took place in the Dawlish area with both up and down lines replaced. On 11 December 2005 EWS No 66043 stands on the down line while replacement of the up track was undertaken through the station area at Dawlish. *Author*

Right: In recent years the station at Dawlish has become very tatty, mainly due to a lack of investment in repairs compounded by a constant battering from the elements. However in 2006 part repainting and refurbishment took place under a joint First Great Western and Network Rail scheme. Viewed from the down platform, Class 150/2 No 150246 slows for the station stop forming the 10.18 Paignton–Exmouth service via Exeter St Davids on 9 June 2005. Due to the curvature of the platform at Dawlish and the Health & Safety requirement for trains to stop on the straight of the platform, stopping services on the up platform pull up towards the London end of the station and not under the canopy, this does cause slight problems during inclement weather. *Author*

Left: From 1 April 2006 the franchise operator for West of England rail services changed. With the introduction of the expanded Greater Western franchise, this encompassed the former Thames, Wessex and Great Western franchises into one larger global operation. To mark the end of the Wessex franchise which existed from 2001 to 2006, local management arranged for a headboard to be carried on some services during the final few days under Wessex control. The very last Wessex westbound service, the 22.24 Exmouth–Paignton was formed of Central Trains-liveried Class 158 No 158794 and two Class 153 'Bubble' cars Nos 153329 and 153369. The last Wessex-operated train is seen at Dawlish, complete with headboard. *Author*

Above: Views of the railway between Dawlish and Kennaway Tunnel can be achieved from numerous locations on Lea Mount or from a footbridge close to the tunnel portal. This afternoon view is from the footpath from the Teignmouth Road giving access to Lea Mount, and is taken above the rooftops of the train paralleling Marine Parade. The town's pier or landing stage is used in summer months for bay trips. This view of Class 180s Nos 180114 and 180104, forming the 14.35 Paddington–Plymouth on 3 August 2004, shows just how close the railway and station are to the sea. *Author*

Right: The view looking from Lea Mount towards Dawlish station can only be described as one of the most popular vantage points for trains traversing the Sea Wall. Several different levels of walkway allow a near-endless range of viewpoints and, aided by different choices of lenses, the views can be varied. This classic morning view from midway up the cliff path shows Class 40 No 40145 passing Dawlish powering 'The Whistling Pixie' tour from Ealing Broadway to Penzance on 28 August 2006. *Author*

Left: The view from the footbridge which crosses the line by the portal of the 209yd long Kennaway Tunnel is well suited for westbound or down trains. In the morning the sunlight is on the sea side, while in the afternoon the sun bears over to the land side. Both offer some excellent views of the bay. Although not favoured by some enthusiasts the Virgin Voyager fleet is very photogenic, displaying the silver, red and yellow colour scheme. With changes in the CrossCountry franchise to be announced in 2007 this colour scheme could well change. With its first-class car leading (identifiable by the yellow Dellner coupling cover), set No 221124 *Charles Lindbergh* heads west on 4 September 2004 forming the 06.43 Dundee–Newquay service. *Author*

Right: Making a rousing departure from Dawlish on 28 February 2005, ex-Great Western 'King' No 6024 *King Edward I* pilots 'Manor' No 7802 *Bradley Manor* with 'The Staite Pullman', the 07.40 Victoria–Paignton private charter formed of the full VSOE Pullman passenger formation. The VSOE Pullman usually operates one public charter duty each year to the West Country, in addition to private specials or special hire contracts. The VSOE, when powered by modern traction, is usually operated by EWS Class 67s. *Author*

Above: During the summer of 2004 Virgin Trains hired four Class 67s on each peak summer Saturday to power leased Mk2 passenger stock on the 08.43 Paignton–Preston, 09.55 Paignton–Newcastle, 07.08 York–Paignton and the 09.51 Preston–Paignton, strengthening these trains as Voyager stock could not cope with passenger demand. On 31 July 2004, No 67027 *Rising Star* passes along Marine Parade emerging from Kennaway Tunnel forming the 08.43 Paignton–Preston service. *Author*

Right: The classic Sea Wall view at Dawlish, a correctly formed 2+8 First Great Western HST set with power cars Nos 43028 and 43033 heads towards Kennaway Tunnel as viewed from Lea Mount on 31 July 2004 while forming the 07.15 Paddington–Paignton service. *Author*

Left: It is worth comparing this and the previous illustration and see how not only the trains have changed in the Marine Parade view of Dawlish. Most of the property in the road has changed, new buildings have been erected, the foliage has grown up on the east side of the town, and car street parking has now changed to angular layout. This view was taken on 6 May 1988 and shows 'large logo' Class 50 No 50015 *Valiant* departing from the Dawlish station stop while forming the 06.45 Swindon–Penzance service. Today, the equivalent of this train is a Bristol Temple Meads–Penzance service formed of a single Class 158. It is interesting to note that timekeeping on the Bristol-Dawlish-Penzance route is much the same today as it was in the days of locomotive-hauled stopping services. *Author*

Right: The early morning light is always good for an up train emerging from Kennaway Tunnel and heading towards Dawlish. This view taken on 20 June 1978 shows the 08.01 Paignton–Paddington service powered by No 50049 *Defiance* slowing for the station call. At this time the semaphore signal was still in use, located by the footbridge and a considerable number of concrete and wooden seats were provided for the public to sit and enjoy the views of Lyme Bay. Today just three bent-up metal seats remain on this section of the wall. This is a view that has changed little over the years, except for growth of the vegetation on Lea Mount and the repainting into bright colours of the buildings behind the train. *Author*

Left: One of the more stunning views of the railway traversing the Dawlish Sea Wall is this at Horse Cove, also known as Shell Cove, showing a train emerging from the 66yd long Clarke Tunnel and skirting around the headland towards the longest of the five tunnels between Dawlish and Teignmouth, Parsons Tunnel at 512yds. In the background one can see Dawlish station and a view is possible right the way along the wall to the curve into Dawlish Warren at Langstone Cliff. The best time to capture trains at this location is around 14.00 in the height of the summer, when as much light as possible is available on the side of the train without too much of the tunnel portal being in shade. Class 57/6 No 57605 *Totnes Castle* hauls First Great Western powercar No 43124, a TGS vehicle, and powercar No 43189 on a stock transfer move from Bristol St Philip's Marsh to Laira on 4 July 2005. *Author*

Right: The view from the top of the gardens on Lea Mount once offered a view of trains emerging from Coryton Tunnel. Today, however, trees and bushes have grown up and almost obstruct this view. The picturesque Coryton Cove is a popular bathing location and is usually a little quieter than the main beach area. In July 1966, an up service powered by a 'Warship' diesel-hydraulic passes a neat line of allotments, a once-common feature along the side of railway lines. *Peter Gray*

Above: The view looking towards Teignmouth from Parsons Tunnel is always pleasing, and this point officially starts the Teignmouth Sea Wall section. The path can be accessed by using Smugglers Lane in Holcombe. On a misty 6 April 2002 morning, EWS Class 66/0 No 66189 approaches Parsons Tunnel hauling ten china-clay slurry tanks as the 08.33 Burngullow–Crewe. This train was destined for the paper mill at Irvine in Ayrshire. *Author*

Left: The use of Wessex Trains, now First Great Western Class 143 railbus units has never been common west of Exeter, but examples are recorded from time to time, mainly operating Exeter-Paignton services. In the long term it is projected more will find work in the West of England. Set No 143613 emerges from the western portal of Parsons Tunnel on 6 April 2002, forming the 10.54 Exmouth–Paignton service. This area around the tunnel mouth, where a small sea inlet exists, is often the scene of wash-outs in adverse weather, and 'rock armour' has been placed by the tunnel to reduce the effects of rough seas. *Author*

Above: Mid-way along the Teignmouth Sea Wall between Parsons Tunnel and Teignmouth is Sprey Point, a small outcrop of land which today carries a 'Welcome to Teignmouth' sign. This small landmass enables some slightly wider views of trains passing along the Teignmouth wall; however, many of the views in this area today have been spoilt by 'rock shields' placed between the rail tracks and cliffs to avoid the possibility of rock falls landing on the line. On 20 July 2002, Super (tilting) Voyager No 221126 *Captain Robert Scott* passes under the down signal gantry at Sprey Point with the 06.05 Derby–Paignton service. *Author*

Left: The vista from Sprey Point looking towards Teignmouth is a splendid view, with the Parish church of Teignmouth, St Michaels, clearly visible and the rolling hills of Shaldon in the distance. An original-liveried HST, led by power car No 43022 rounds the curve away from Teignmouth on 5 July 1984 forming the 07.25 Plymouth–Paddington service. When this view was taken the mechanical signalbox located at the west end of Teignmouth station was still open, with the box's down outer lower-quadrant semaphore home signal showing 'clear' just past the rear of the train. *Author*

Above: The Skew Bridge (technically East Cliff Walk) crossing the railway at the Teignmouth end of the Sea Wall always offers an attractive backdrop to photographs. Pictures at this point are best taken in the morning when the light is at its best. On 14 August 2004, Arriva-liveried Class 158 Nos 158830 and 158838 form the 06.10 Penzance–Manchester Piccadilly and Pembroke Dock service. Upon the franchise changes in early 2006, Arriva Trains Wales ceased to operate west of Bristol. *Author*

Above: A small earth mound adjacent to the Teignmouth end of the Teignmouth Sea Wall path offers some pleasant views of trains in this area. Here the photographer was treated to a lineup of trains parked on the up track during engineering work at Dawlish on 20 November 2005, when the route between Exeter and Newton Abbot was closed. In this view, taken mid-morning, EWS Class 66/0 Nos 66052 and 66186 stand either end of a track-re-laying machine at the head of a spoil train, while other engineering trains are spread out along the wall towards Parsons Tunnel. *Author*

Left: The area around Teignmouth station is where the railway turns slightly inland before progressing west alongside the River Teign. Teignmouth station has two platforms, but until the 1960s sported a small goods yard located to the rear of the up platform and accessed by a set of trailing points located tight to the road bridge directly at the London end of the station and visible in this view. At the London end of Teignmouth station four bridges cross the railway; one passes over the station platforms, one directly at the end of the platforms, a private road bridge and footpath link the council car park with the sea front and finally there is the famous 'skew' bridge on the curve of the Teignmouth Sea Wall. This view is taken from the footbridge looking back towards the station. EWS Class 67 No 67003 passes non-stop through the station on 14 August 2004 powering Virgin Trains' summer Saturday relief 09.05 Paignton–Newcastle service. Sadly, this holiday relief train departed from Paignton too early for many hotel-based passengers, who were unable to have breakfast, check out of their accommodation and make their way to the station. However, on its way north the train picked up many passengers from other areas. *Author*

Right: The view looking down on the railway and Teignmouth Sea Wall from the 'skew' bridge is another of the classic views, used on many official Great Western Railway, British Railways and private-sector advertisements. It is not easy to stand on this bridge to capture pictures, as it is on an angle, has quite high sides and foliage has grown up on an adjacent embankment. However, the use of a short step ladder usually allows the photographer the right view, although the locals, holiday makers and even the police often look a little bemused. South West Trains Class 159s Nos 159019 and 159006 round the curve into Teignmouth forming the 08.41 Basingstoke–Paignton service on 14 August 2004. In the middle distance of this view Sprey Point can be seen on the left, with the entrance to Parsons Tunnel behind. The little stack of rock at the end of the headland is Shag Rock, while in the far distance is the area between Exmouth and Budleigh Salterton. To the left of the six-car Class 159 is some of the recently-erected rock protection fencing, built to protect the railway from rock and sand falls. *Author*

Above: Just to the west of Teignmouth is the Port of Teignmouth, operated by Associated British Ports. This facility is sadly not rail connected. Directly after the port, with the railway now skirting the River Teign, the line curves below Shaldon Bridge. This is the A379 Dawlish/Teignmouth to Torquay/Paignton road and offers a good viewpoint for trains travelling in both directions. In more recent times, in the quest for safety fences have been erected along the waterside wall of the railway which has slightly spoilt some photographs, but careful positioning of the subject still allows good views to be taken. A Midland Mainline-operated HST, led by power car No 43052 with No 43104 on the rear, approaches Shaldon Bridge on 1 July 2006 forming the 07.24 Manchester–Newquay Virgin Trains service. *Author*

Left: The view looking west from Shaldon Bridge enables trains rounding the tight curve at Teignmouth boat yard to be captured. On 1 July 2006, the 08.52 Penzance–Paddington service heads towards Teignmouth led by power car No 43156. Views from this location are best achieved during the morning when the light is on the estuary side. *Author*

Above: Between Teignmouth and Hackney (Newton Abbot) the railway skirts the banks of the River Teign. Little access is available to the line on this section, but some views from the A381 Teignmouth-Newton Abbot road are possible. Views looking across the River Teign from the Shaldon-Combeinteignhead-Newton Abbot Road are also possible. Midway between Teignmouth and Newton Abbot near the village of Bishopsteignton a footpath crosses fields to a footbridge over the railway leading to the waterside; this offers some views of trains, but undergrowth has grown up to such an extent that pictures such as this of 'Peak' No 45106 leading the 08.55 Newquay–Manchester Piccadilly on 7 July 1984 are no longer possible. During the 1980s a number of long-distance holiday relief services were operated by the then InterCity Cross-Country arm and shifted thousands and thousands of passengers each weekend, with many trains formed of up to 13 Mk1s able to seat up to 800 people, compared with a four-car 'Voyager' of today with seating for just 188! *Author*

Right: The view looking down at the River Teign from the Teignmouth-Newton Abbot Road provides an excellent vista. On 4 August 1967 a three-car Class 118 DMU heads towards Newton Abbot, with the bridge from which the above view was taken visible on the far left. *Peter Gray*

Above: A carefully chosen date and time to visit the banks of the River Teign near Wear Farm, close to Hackney, when it was high tide and the sun was in the right position produced this stunning image of Swindon-built B-B 'Warship' No D803 *Formidable*, powering west with the down 'Devonian' on 23 June 1960. The light at this location in the early evening is at its best. Today this view is near impossible, with lineside growth and problems with access. *Peter Gray*

Right: This wonderful Great Western signal gantry was located at Hackney, east of Newton Abbot and controlled entry into Hackney Yard as well as the main line. On 16 June 1967, North British Locomotive Co-built Class 22 B-B diesel-hydraulic No D6320 heads west into the yard, leading a long rake of general merchandise wagons. The NBL Type 2 was not a hugely successful locomotive, and in common with all the diesel-hydraulic classes faced early withdrawal following the BRB's decision to concentrate on the diesel-electric transmission system. *Peter Gray*

Above: One of the classic railway views in the West Country, looking over Newton Abbot station from the west end, showing the through lines on the far left, the station with four through platform lines in the centre and the workshops, sidings and diesel running depot on the right. On the far right, adjacent to the former goods shed, which by the 1970s was the home of publisher David & Charles, are three preserved LNER coaches. This picture, dated 23 January 1975, is very significant, as it is the first ever picture of a High Speed Train operating in the West Country, when prototype HST set No 252001 formed a trial and press special from London to Plymouth, demonstrating the operating potential of HST trains over the Devon banks. The full 2+9 set worked from London to Plymouth and then a return trip to Newton Abbot before returning to London. It is seen taking a clear signal towards Aller Junction and then Dainton Bank. *Peter Gray*

Above: Newton Abbot station today is but a shadow of the past. Following 1980s rationalisation and closure of the depot and workshop facilities adjacent to the station a few years before, the station is now left with just three platform faces and a bay which is only used for stabling purposes in an emergency. Taken during the period of rationalisation, after the through lines had been removed on the left, Class 118 DMU set No P466 departs west with the 11.50 Newton Abbot to Paignton service on 2 October 1984. To the left of the train is Newton Abbot West signalbox, which once sported 153 levers and was finally demolished on 2 May 1987. The signal gantry to the right, which is of 1960s BR construction, is now 'preserved' by Newton Abbot Council and erected on an industrial estate adjacent to the station, but its long-term survival is in some doubt due to local redevelopment. Today this view from the dual carriageway overbridge is hardly recognisable. *Author*

Above: The area around Newton Abbot was always a hub of railway life. The depot adjacent to the station was home for a sizeable steam and later modern traction fleet, including many of the well-loved 'Warship' diesel-hydraulic locomotives which replaced steam traction from Western Region crack express services in the early 1960s. Displaying the stunning Western Region maroon livery, with a matching rake of Mk1 stock, 'Warship' No D869 *Zest* pauses at Newton Abbot on 4 June 1967 with an inter-regional express bound for Birmingham. The main station buildings at Newton Abbot, visible above the locomotive, are still intact today and the ground floor houses the First Great Western ticket office. Just to the London end of Newton Abbot station a junction on the up side takes a single-line spur to Heathfield. This is now only used for occasional EWS-operated china-clay traffic and the very infrequent overnight stabling of the Royal Train when Her Majesty the Queen or Prince Charles visits the West Country. *Author*

Above: Until 2004 several Royal Mail post services operated each weekday to and from various points in the north of the UK and Plymouth, bringing a change to the usual passenger traffic to the Sea Wall route. In later years these trains were powered by EWS Class 67s, but occasionally a Class 47 from the previous era could be found. On 15 July 2002, Class 67 No 67005 *Queen's Messenger*, which is now painted in 'Royal Claret' livery, rounds the tight curve off the Plymouth line at Aller Divergence with the daily 17.23 Plymouth–Newcastle Low Fell service formed of five vans and a PCV set on the rear. *Author*

Above: Directly to the west of Newton Abbot is Aller; in railway terms this was once Aller Junction, where the twin tracks of the Plymouth and Paignton lines split, but today the location is known as Aller divergence, as the physical split of the lines is at Newton Abbot and only the direction change is made at Aller. Approaching Aller from the Plymouth line and dropping down Dainton incline towards Langford Bridge, EWS Class 66/0 No 66071 heads the 08.33 Burngullow–Crewe china-clay service on 13 April 2002. The location at Langford Bridge offers good all-round views of the line for most of the day, but following local industrial estate development the road is now very busy and can be quite dangerous. *Author*

Above: During the track rationalisation of West Country routes in the 1980s associated with the West of England re-signalling project, it is a wonder the section between Newton Abbot and Aller remained a four-track railway, but thankfully it did and it offers some pleasant photographic views. Traversing the down Plymouth line and approaching Aller Divergence, Freightliner Heavy Haul No 66622 heads the second portion of the twice-weekly Hope to Moorswater cement train on 9 June 2005. This train operates as one full load to Hackney yard and then operates forward to Moorswater as two sections due to weight restrictions traversing the South Devon banks. *Author*

Left: Langford Bridge on the Plymouth line at Aller, affords an excellent view back to Newton Abbot. On 25 February 2004, then un-named Class 57/6 No 57604 starts the climb of Dainton powering the 09.18 Old Oak Common–Plymouth test run. On the rear of the train is Class 47 No 47832. A number of test runs were carried out around this time to trial the recently delivered Class 57s, which were ordered by First Great Western to replace Class 47s on the Paddington–Penzance overnight sleeper services. *Author*

Right: With a sighting plate on the rear of the lower-quadrant semaphore signal protecting the then Aller Junction off the Paignton line, 'Peak' Class 45/0 No 45014 *The Cheshire Regiment* slows for the junction layout and approaches the Aller Break bridge on 5 July 1984 powering a Paignton–Leicester return excursion train formed of 13 blue and grey-liveried Mk1 coaches. *Author*

Above: A farm bridge which crosses close to Aller divergence offers some excellent views of trains on all lines, but again growth of lineside vegetation is spoiling some views. In perfect afternoon sun, ex-GWR 'Castle' No 5051 *Earl Bathurst* opens the regulator after seeing a 'proceed' signal protecting Newton Abbot while pulling off the Paignton line on 1 August 2004, powering one of the timetabled summer Sunday 'Torbay Express' charters which operate most summers between Bristol Temple Meads and Kingswear on the Paignton & Dartmouth Railway. The area to the left of the fourth carriage of the train was the location of Aller Junction signalbox which closed in April 1987. *Author*